Spread Thick

poems by

Sara Triana

Finishing Line Press
Georgetown, Kentucky

Spread Thick

ACKNOWLEDGMENTS

"Spread Thick", "As in, Deactivate", "The Last Time", and "On the Afternoon
of November 6" were previously published in BEATIFIC Magazine, Winter
2021, Volume 1, Number 1.

"All This Time Her Bones" was previously published on The Waking by
Ruminate Magazine.

"To Raise Children Today is to Engage in Magical Thinking" was previously
published in *Wondrous World: Poems That Spark Magic* by Other Worldly
Women Press.

Publisher: Leah Huete de Maines
Editor: Christen Kincaid
Cover Art and Design: Rachel Gonzales
Author Photo: Chip Gillespie

Order online: www.finishinglinepress.com
also available on amazon.com

Author inquiries and mail orders:
Finishing Line Press
P. O. Box 1626
Georgetown, Kentucky 40324
U. S. A.

Table of Contents

My Ideal Readers ...1

It All Happened So Quickly ...2

Before ...3

PART I PANDEMIC SPRING

On The First Day With Mangos ...7

On The Sixth Night, A Love Letter...10

In The Silent Hours We Guessed The Names Of Birds ...12

Greetings, Late March ...14

If All You Want Is To Be With Us ...16

A Month Inside ...18

Late April Resolution ...19

Say When ...20

The Shape Of Life ...22

The Revolution Won't Be Tweeted ...23

Seasick ...25

The Weight Of You ...27

PART II PANDEMIC SUMMER

A Home To Be Sick For ...31

As In, Will There Be A Fourth ...34

Everything's Missable ...35

Spread Thick ...37

Southern Baptist ...38

Apologetics ...39

The One About The Wall ...40

You Won't Die Now. You Will Watch ...42

Dear Mom And Dad ...43

Shutdown Love Song ...45

Poem That Runs Through My Life ...46

Housewifery And Politics ...47

What Is My History Of Reading Poetry ...48

Tell Us About When We Were Little ...49

It's A Classic Will They Or Won't They ...50

Radical Tenderness // The Game ...51

Tenth Anniversary Sentimental ...54
As If Asked How To Keep The Light On ...55
The Bon Bons Are Your Birth Right ...56
A Waste ... 58
As If One Had The Right To Complain ...59
As If Asked Who I Am Writing For ...61
As In, I've Held Blizzards Upside Down ...62
As If The Summer Would Never End ...63

PART III PANDEMIC FALL
As In, How Are You Going To Leave When They're Still Here ...69
September 29 Wishlist ...70
Milk And Flowers...71
As If I Had My Own Plan, As If I Had Not Come To Get Pregnant...72
People Keep Knocking On My Door To Lecture Me ...73
As In, Deactivate ...74
All This Time Her Bones ...75
Late October Road Trip, The Election Has Begun ...76
Hope, A Practice ...79
Coming To Take It ...80
November 2, 2020 ...83
Certitudes, November 4 ...84
On The Afternoon Of November 6 ...85
"Resistance Is Fertile" ...86
The Errand ...88
Everyone's In On It ...89
We Mulled Over How To Make It Not A Lost Year...90
To Raise Children Today Is To Engage In Magical Thinking ...91
P.S. ...92

*To the ones we lost, in every way, during the pandemic
and to the ones who lost them*

In memory of Karen Ruse, Jack Sheppard, and David Naugle

MY IDEAL READERS

to the slow talkers
men who like cats
people who know how to roast an eggplant
and the ones who set up jam circles

to girls with mullets
bashful actuaries
mothers and daughters who speak after work
step-dads who cry
and the regretfully assimilated

to french-braiders
folx
gay teenage bakers
the estranged
and men who sing bass

to community gardeners
and people whose jokes die in their mouths

to the retired art teachers guild
wise old children
and the glubby-voiced

I threaded this and knotted it for you.

IT ALL HAPPENED SO QUICKLY

Every date looks old.
When was that written?
Yesterday,
so long ago.

BEFORE

found poems from morning pages

March 3, 2020

I would be with someone
who was at the same mall
as the infected person.

March 6, 2020

One night writing retreat.
The baby sleeps. I brought her.

I cannot believe I have poems I like
because I cannot write poetry.

I can't hear the music.
Does the music come?

I read some poems that seemed like conversations with children.
Grab-a-napkin stories.

It's my life but I can't see it in stanzas.
I hardly write about my own mom and dad.

PART I

PANDEMIC SPRING

ON THE FIRST DAY WITH MANGOS

In the first days when some of us
began to take the virus seriously and too late
as every country bloomed
with positives tests,

I bought an armload of plants
and mangos, pineapple, and limes.
We planted the seedlings in our garden beds

spread compost and moved stones
to form a path,
I turned 33 that night so we shared a steak
and built a fire in the backyard
and as it cracked we realized

how close the virus was
how long it had already been here
how fast it moved.

I cried and said please don't sing to me
not with this gnawing in my heart

because with every breath I wonder who will stop to visit Granny
and what she will breathe in
and I can't blow candles out like this

but we lit the candle anyway
and Clementine sang the loudest
with her face shining like a gift.

Every day she asked if the sickness is over
and what she meant was can we see our family.

And every day I read the news from Italy
and what I meant was show me our future.

Each night that first week
I would put the baby to sleep
fasten my helmet and glide into the quiet
neighborhood on my bike.

The roads were not full of people coming home from work
because the people never went.
They didn't pick up dinner, didn't pick up the kids

didn't swing by the store or pop into the art opening.
They didn't make it to the gym or to practice or rehearsal.

In the first days, the paths were quiet
except for sunset beds, rabbit thumps, and mowers.

Eventually, I would find someone
out for a run, out for a ride
to walk the dog, to stretch the legs
to talk on the phone away from the kids.

Sometimes, to the lonely, I will give my beauty queen smile.
I know what it says. It says I'm a safe one.
But to most I just call "I'm on your left!" or I nod.

Even back then, when it hardly felt real
something was already different
cracked like the pavement that jostled my bike

and the threat of *what if* tied my tongue
because I don't know how to say *I see you, mister sad eyes*
and *don't breathe on me* at the same time.

I don't know how to say
Hello neighbor while I'm imagining your saliva
and sweat racing through the air.

And I know they felt afraid too because
even with my biggest *you can trust me* smile
even with my chirpiest *on your left please if you don't mind*
most people wouldn't meet my eyes

and they were holding their breath too
with a gnawing in their chest too
afraid for their own grannies when I rode by

and I've never felt less human
than when I passed them without inhaling
and I've never felt more human
more porous and afraid.

All I want all day is to hear
Clementine parrot "I can be brave and afraid
at the same time" over and over and sing to me
in our garden bed
fat with mondo grass and mango peels.

In our first cloistered days, everything was still plump
like a pantry of snacks
and only our dreams were lean
as we all held our breath and waited.

ON THE SIXTH NIGHT, A LOVE LETTER

It's on the sixth night that I want
to write a love letter to La Cocina de Roberto
our neighborhood taqueria

stuff in hundred dollar bills I don't have and say
Please resurrect. Please rise
on the other side with carnitas and be okay.

Really it's more than that
more than the street tacos and plantains
Roberto's mango habanero smile.

It's about your old best friend
digging into a sauce-sloppy torta.
It's about how the torta mended all wounds.

Why did the adults in the room
deny this was coming to my family
but in private rooms book jets,

drop stocks, and warn their sons
how it would rip through like 1918?
Just the flu—

I would have filled ocean liners with tests
taken everyone's temps
locked the doors and tipped all the staff

for the months to come, if I knew
what was coming. If I knew about
the live-streamed funerals and weddings.

If I knew no one would walk
across the stage, that the cost
would be closeness chest to chest

cheek to cheek
and that tomorrow our plans include, yet again
reading the news and not leaving this beautiful island.

IN THE SILENT HOURS WE GUESSED THE NAMES OF BIRDS

The time we all tucked into our homes
for safekeeping, when the streets shushed
the chef's calls and the cook's retort
the playgrounds, cathedrals,
and the locker rooms went quiet.

These things turned up:
birdsong and the rainfall
the slup-glup sounds of infants drinking milk
keyboard clicks and paper rustle
sirens and rumors
and the daily counts.

In the silent hours, we guessed the names of birds
we had never stopped to hear before.
We knelt in our houses and said
the creeds from our couches in screen glow.

Yesterday in the pause we were witnesses
to the crouch and prowl of our cat in the grass watching
a baby warbler bobbing around with new wings
not knowing yet the mechanics of flight.

Amelie, our cat, readied for the pounce
and we screamed to *stop stop absolutely stop.*

The mama warbler with her yellow breast swooped
through with a call that was shrill and clear
as her baby bird bobbed and hopped away
and we scooped up our prowler and scuttled her inside.

Today I sat across the same yard
from my father tired in his bones and nerves
from hours cleaning up the Costco.

We chatted like it was normal to sit ten feet apart.
As if it were normal for him to drive thirty miles
to bring hand sanitizer and Lysol.

Then, in a white blonde flash, my three year old
dashed across the wet grass
with a Topo Chico for Papi's lap
as we all screamed *stop stop absolutely stop.*

Don't you know, we thought shrill and clear,
he can't stay home? He is essential.
Don't you know Papi could / we all could have it
the thing in the air?

My baby hopped away into my arms
and cried deep and loud while
we explained it all again, although I still
don't understand what happened to life
as we knew it.

Later, she and I buried the tiny yellow breasted chat
caught between persistent sharp teeth and strong jaws
and we slipped down the street for a walk.

I can tell you the ripple water in the stream
never roared so loud as on this day at dusk
when we raced our flowers down, petaled
drifters on the little chime waves
and the echo bubbles blubbed under a still grey sky
where no planes fly.

GREETINGS, LATE MARCH

I'm writing to report that the honeysuckle
is beginning to blossom trumpets of a second coming
The air is plumply perfumed and paused.
It is still. No cars pass while I do laps on my bike

I cruise past golf courses
where disease does not exist
passing golfers still slapping
each other's hammy shoulders.

It feels like Harvey is back at our doors,
hurtling up from the shore and the flood waters
won't quit creeping up the cash green hills
of the country club course in little warm waves.

But it's not the unrelenting rain, the dirty side of the Gulf this time.
It's the weight of our words, the spatter of syntax
the particles of our prose hanging in a cloud of conversation
that's boarding up windows
closing our stores, cancelling class.

Our discourse, our hymns and hoorahs, are possibly poison
and we don't know how to say hello anymore.

Even so—the honeysuckle
is beginning to blossom here
yellow and white, it smells just like you remember.

The monarchs and the swallowtails have returned.
They still snag each other in the air
flap on the ground to craft their little changelings
out of a violent slap and winged thwack.

I'm reading an old textbook of creation myths
and I'll admit I felt dismayed to find
that mine is just one of a million—.

In the beginning, the same air
that curls coughs into our pink lungs
is also sweet along the vines arching
wrapping their tendrils and tomorrows blooms around the gates,
around the old stone walls and the mildewed pine fences
that line our little kingdoms.

IF ALL YOU WANT IS TO BE WITH US

At the close of March,
I want to rub my eyes the way I cry:
a swift abolition of every tear.

Why can't I run into the coffee shop that knows me
to my friend Rachel? We could weep together
like storybook women but we don't know

what we can touch anymore or who.
Some people are nervous to kiss their children,
washing their own hands raw. We are afraid

to touch our parents and afraid of all they touch.
I've never stood at the foot
of a global death count for any reason.

Can you count to thirty-seven thousand
and eighty three?
How do you grasp the numbers?

I compare them to towns I have loved.
It's as if all the lights went out in Nacogdoches.

Where do I put this death?
Does it splash into the bowls
of stew I ladle for my little ones?

Do I leave a trail of it along our path through the woods—
crumbs that could lead us back
to homes that remember?

Beneath it all, I hear this liturgical chant:
God wants to be *with* us?
Then be with us on the couch, whoever you are

and in the driveway where, forehead bowed on the wheel
it almost looks like we're praying
not scrounging for certainty

not pondering how to rebuild something from dust.
How was that done once?
And what happens to our plans?

Come on then and be with us
in our varied ways of weeping
for what was prismatic
for what became pixelated
for the virtual grief
for my niece on a screen
and the last time I held her
letting her snooze on my chest
not knowing what would pass
and how long it would be
until I could nuzzle my nose into her red hair again.

Come on and let's count backward
from thirty-seven thousand and eighty-three
grab hands, and find a way to get back home.

A MONTH INSIDE

And now we wait
in the in-between, in early April
halting. Shut down and shut in.

Liminal, it's a word I hear and pause upon
every time, like *boundaries*, I'm learning
to use it. Giving it to you.

Here we are, living in the liminal
together, with every calendared piece of our life
slashed through, scribbled out.

We turned the page mid-March and found
a place between our plans:
a spread of unfilled boxes
that continues to unfold.

Daughters, our lives have become blank pages
suddenly and universally
and all I can tell you is that this is everywhere
every calendar is a relic, *shutdown.*

We lose our words for the future tense
one by one: *plans, dates,*
getaway.

Today, between picture books and block building
I'm brewing a new truth: that
our real life is not on pause.

That this is our real life, quieted,
contained in our home, our yard,
a still life. We are waiting, living through

this: *pandemic.* Another new one
for us. Slowed—we are home, still
waking and growing here.
Showing up, now *essential.*

LATE APRIL RESOLUTION

This is the moment I decide not to be an artist.

I made the plunge.
I said I'm here

and this is the way I write words
the way I feel in buckets and splashes.

It's all too real now.
the costs of being an artist

are a maxed out credit card
and somehow my blood pulses to the beat of

buy my book

buy my book

buy my book

I tied my boat to this dock
but now let me wrestle the rope

work it in reverse and set free
wander the water and wave

goodbye!
I can write poems for free

float on the grass, lay in the breeze
braid heads of blonde hair

and no ones gotta buy my books no more.
Don't like and don't subscribe.

SAY WHEN

We are going down to the coffee shop to celebrate its third birthday.

We'll wear shoes. We'll wear masks
and glance sideways at bare faces.

We heard our taqueria will be there with free tacos
and I hope the green sauce comes, too.

I put on a shirt, eye the outline of my breasts in the mirror.
Am I brave enough for my own softness?

I imagine my family crossing the parking lot
with smiling eyes as lattes are poured over ice outside.

Our friends will be there, every one of them
and it will almost be like a reunion.
It will almost be like saying "See! Good things are still happening!"

I wear a bra.

But when we get there the eyes all belong to strangers.
Even if my friends had come, we wouldn't hug.
We calculate the space between bodies
and side-eye bare faces.

I order the coffees and tacos to-go
while the kids jingle jangle around the car.

They'll say
mom didn't grab enough free tacos
I'll say *let's go* and think *this was a dumb idea.*
We cannot hug and no ones here and we'll never see anyone again.

And when will I ever need a bra now?
Will I wear one at Thanksgiving?
Will we be chest to chest then?

Or on Christmas will we gather at tables pushed together
with my cousins at the volunteer fire department?
Will we still be coughing then?

Who will hold me and when?
Until then, no thank you.
Unless I'm on a bike.

THE SHAPE OF LIFE

Three months into the pandemic
I don't understand the shape of my life anymore.
Time is blobby, undefined
borderless, undifferentiated.

And if there is no heaven
And there is no one to save
And if there is no yeast for the bread
And there is nothing to sell
And if there is only each breath
And if there is not
And if the ballots are lost
And the votes aren't counted
And there's no party on Christmas
So no one sees our crowns or cares
If the beach collapses into the sea before New Year's
And I keep scrolling but find no bottom
And if our bellies stay filled but the guest room stays empty

How will I know day from day?
I don't remember the creation tale, its compass—
How we fix what was broken.
Where do I go from here? And what do I redeem?

How long does this last and how is it measured?
In bites of news on our dinner plates.
In paychecks and checkmarks on lists.
I will rake the pine needles

pile them on kitchen scraps in the compost bin
choose an empty day to scoop it out
with the scurry of roaches and toads
the quick retreat of earthworms
turn it, pile it back in, wait a month, and do it again.

THE REVOLUTION WON'T BE TWEETED

Who needs to be on Twitter
for the snark and rage
and signals and wit?

You can read a newspaper
read striations on a green tomato
and marvel that an orange colored
Northern Cardinal—a rare variety—
came to witness the beanstalk
came to notice how nothing grows
in the sandy spot of the garden
where the downspout flows
where the rainwater deposits silt
and the squirrel-gnawed cores of pine cones.

It is enough to say
yes, tear down the Confederacy
and her statues and her supremacy
and make room for us all to
plant our gardens
to gather wet faces off the ground
to fire off guffaws like gun shots
into the activated air between us
and pass our breath back and forth
with the trees.

And where does all this knowing go?
What summit does the snark propose to climb?
Where are we going sidelong upon a smirk
If not door to door
If not car to car with a box of food
If not into our paint and prose?

It is enough to say
first, tear it down in me.
Root it out. Disrupt me—
every plant in my soil yank them

without relent until the pest is out.
Gather—every broad-petalled yellow flower
the withered tangles of vines
and bore-eaten hollow stems.
Pile them in the yard
with the old cartoons as tinder
And burn down the system that presses cheeks
and chests against the rough cut of concrete
until long past breath can come.

SEASICK

My mouth checks for fevers all day
without thought or intention
and night is when the children
find their way to me down the path of night lights.
They open the quilt like the hatch
and climb in so that our dreams might meet.

And even there in a dream land
where it snows and where animals
are friends who speak

even there I am the mother.
Like in all their games, they say
"I'll be the baby
and mom you're the mommy."

Sharing a pillow and the right
side of the bed they will sink deeper
into sleep and I will float
upon it lighter
with their legs checking
in with mine. They make sure
I haven't slipped away
to another bed
another dream of deeper sleep.

It is the warm legs in the night
that will first tell me she is sick
and then my hand
will check her cheeks
will check her forehead and neck
and then the legs again
and confirm, yes,
we don't need numbers
for this heat.

I fall asleep in my own fever of thought
thinking of droplets and culprits and coughs
knowing that if one is sick
we all will sink by our shared beds
shared cups and slices of pizza
and the dozens of daytime kisses
that sew us five together
like a sea of dreams.

THE WEIGHT OF YOU

The weight of you matters more than I remembered.

Who are we to each other unembodied?
Who are we without the space between us
gently hissing through your nose in and out, your ocean breath?

The matter of you is a part of us, as much as memories and mind.

Who are we without the depth of you, front to back, without the velvet of my
skin and my quiet listening? The way you would watch me held a weight I can't
feel through screens.

I want the deep crease of your nose unflattened, unfiltered, the fullness of you.
I want the hair on your arm to stand up.
Give me goosebumps.
Read me the stories on your knuckles.
Let me tell you one with my palms.

It's not just our connection
it's our pressing in
our proximity that resonates.
It's the way we sit—two bodies just mattering in the same room.

Who are we to each other without heat?
Without the summer beating into both of us
the sweat on your shoulders
the sun going down painting our faces in orange and expectation?

Who are we without being split
in the same second by the sudden dark and star smatter—
without the hot dock beneath our legs?

Who are we to each other without our bodies?

Tell me what season it was when we snuck out,
climbed the ladder to meet the moon.

And now, what seasonless span never ends? Give me the date for being multi-dimensional again.

I don't want your texts. Dig in. Hoist me by my ribs into the musk of you. Let fingers find fingers. Inhale me under last light, under smoked shadow.

Don't be a memory. Be dynamic. Be an actual thing in my arms.

Don't read the newsletter. Send a real letter. Lick the seal. Send something of yourself in the crease of the pages. An eyelash, your hand on my knee, the ghost of a groan. Deliver you to me. And read me. Read my thighs. Read my grip.

Land on me.
Hit me with a laugh that blasts my hair back.
Undistance yourself.

Be tangible, a too loud chorus in my ear. Be spit in the air.
Hold out your hand in the space between us saying *look, I'm shaking.*

PART II

PANDEMIC SUMMER

A HOME TO BE SICK FOR

And what if I had known
about the cucumbers, how
heavy they would hang
in the front yard garden

And that we would be the kind
to chop them, crowning
a mountain of green leaf lettuce
and pepper cracked with salty cheese?

Could I have imagined
two pies: blackberry and peach,
my bed-rumbled daughter and me tining the fruit
and flakes of crust for breakfast all July?

Or a morning slow enough to watch
a grasshopper slip from its skeleton
over cups of black coffee
over the purr of cicadas?

And would it have been enough
to know there would be a chest
to call home, a kitchen floor
to dance across with juleps and jazz?

If only I'd heard rumblings of the births
and the bellies, of the milk that
drips down skin to skin.
Had I heard I'd be the best seat

in the house, one day.
Or that we'd spend New Year's
on the beach in the blue afternoon
with shell-covered sandcastles

laughing at how one daughter runs
into the waves
waving her arms behind
like she's holding herself back.

Hold on and head south! What would be
the power of this prophecy? Dreamer—
there is a garden of hostas, hibiscus
and a good dog waiting for you.

Would it have been a balm?
Would the future be the friend I needed?
A messenger of relief confiding,
"love, we don't even believe in hell anymore

or war, or dieting.
The souls have been saved
and we eat pie
and poetry for breakfast."

And if this dream had swelled with the barn swallows in the yard
the caterpillars crawling up the sprawling petunias
the squirrels and the blue jays racing through the wooded backyard
and the meadowlark, and the baby wrens flapping past fat cats—

Had the creamy lime blossoms floated their notes
from the now to the then
to me in my girlhood wishing
through every cold window

for a trumpet peal—
staring out, wanting to run
to grow up but having no hope
of what I could grow into

praying to vanish
in a twinkling
into a golden gated heaven
where I could feel this safe.

If the cucumbers had been foretold
like the second coming I believed in,
if I had found a tiny blue bottle
of that Galveston sand to pour into my palm—

Wouldn't just one of these
have been enough? A real heaven
to have faith in—A horizon
to run headlong into—A home

to be sick for.

AS IN, WILL THERE BE A FOURTH

Inside
my womb are a hundred more lives
and their daily requests for buttered toast

but I'm done.

EVERYTHING'S MISSABLE

Everything's climbable when you're 11 months old: the stairs and the fireplace and the built-in benches on the back deck.

In the spring heat, my third baby, Beatrix, pulls herself up on the bench and wobble-paces with a wide smile as I wade into nostalgia.

We bought this house four years ago because my honey-blonde first baby, Anabelle, found a way to climb up from the yard, up from the wild mess of tall grass, the sun-bleached mulch, the drifts of pine needles, up under the built-in benches onto the deck with a crow of a half-hidden smile.

And I would sign any line as it seemed like a place she'd need another 10 years or more to explore.

In the cool of our first winter in the house, I would lay our second daughter, Clementine, out there on the deck on a yoga mat on her belly where she would lift up her chest, white hair fluttering, and swim her legs in the air, watching me with love letter blue eyes as her sister tugged white blossoms off the azaleas the first time they bloomed for us.

Today my baby Bea paces back and forth across the benches, my only brown-haired girl and I'm not too proud to admit that my heart sung when she slung out of my body. Our labor was over and my joy began right at the top of her elfin brown head.

Every cell of mine remembers their stitching together and stretching but every cell of me startles knowing that I have reached this place: I am a mother with all my births behind me.

And the strangest feeling I have isn't knowing that I have three daughters but realizing that their mother is me: I will be *this figure* for them for their whole lives.

When they think about the things their mother would do and the fruit she would buy and the things she yelled and the way she smelled, it will be the clary sage on my neck and the sweat from an afternoon sorting out the backyard that sings in their nostrils.

I didn't know it would sting, loving them.

And what will they think of this origin story? That mom wanted this house because of the way Anabelle crawled up the deck and that's it.

And she doesn't now, scooch under the benches. She crawls to another world through a screen like I would crawl through books and daydreams. Our mothers are always a place to leave, a home to write to.

I ask her to take a walk with me. She says we've had plenty of walks but she will let me cut her bangs and she will eat my blackberry pie for breakfast.

I want to think of their future laughter in my ears to save me from the fear of losing them. I will dream of their heads tossed back howling, laugh-crying in the shade garden where I raised endless milkweed, hosta, and the sprawling bougainvillea in the mornings of our lives under the pines.

I want to write on every river stone that I lay along the flower bed borders "this is the day we read Silverstein and sloshed red tea out of chipped mugs" or "Bea's first birthday" or "worst fight ever but we lived" and under every root ball I will plant each day's to-do list, our lives check by check coming up like vinca leaves and blossoms.

I know one day the summer heat will summon them at dusk and we will dine beneath the pines where we grew old and fierce and storied. I wish I were better at visiting the future, hanging my hat on what could come up from the ground were cultivating, because everything's missable when you're 33 and your memories are a million planes of you to float upon.

I'm afraid of the sadness to come in the afterlight. I'm afraid of missing them so I feel it now, swim back and feel their peach faces pressed into mine so I'll never have to miss them all at once when they're grown and gone.

In my memory, Anabelle never says we've had plenty of walks and wild and roses. We are always just embarking, just about to sign our names.

SPREAD THICK

Spread me thick across my life like salted butter, like raw honey. Pour me into living, like swirls of coconut cream into curry.

Amplify my aliveness. Turn up the trembling locust song, the weep of toads in the rain. I want to stay here and hear everything.

Cinch me snug to each sensation. Let it punctuate and feel good. Let living hurt. Let loose my past and even let the future flutter away unfettered. Nothing needs me but now. Cancel everything.

Clear my calendar for my days are filled with
simmering pots of sauce
shimmering thoughts and blonde locks
and the silvering head of my father who has stopped by for a long visit on the lawn.

This is my trick to keep from crawling right out of my skin, extinguishing angst with the news, devouring analysis, thinking and thinking but never sprawling out across the rug to let the plucks and hums of harp and guitar set the room abloom and me with it—an eruption of jazz-tinged petals, a wry row of wild rose percussion.

Breathe me into the flow state of being in my body, touching my tongue to the fire, my lips to lips. Let the pucker of existing punch me in the sockets of my jaw, knocked out and seeing stars of how it feels to feel.

Where else would I want to be? I refuse to be scraped thin across the crust. I am thick and never-ending, a napping cat stretched fat and long across the bed with glowing green eyes for spotting rust-colored dragonflies.

Crown me the queen of the moment and at my coronation, play me at a rhythm that reacts to the arrival of hummingbird wings, here to lick the salvia's red blossoms of plenty.

SOUTHERN BAPTIST

You were supposed to be good
Was I raised by believers
Or by wolves

APOLOGETICS

It's not that I need to be convinced. Please don't feel the need to prove it to me. It's simply that I don't believe. It's like the thing in me called *faith in these particular things* just slipped out of my open mouth one night while I was dreaming, leaked onto the pillow and dried so that it was hardly noticeable, a shadow. Then in the spring it was washed out with the deep cleaning, with the great pandemic purge.

THE ONE ABOUT THE WALL

1.

I was raised behind the wall from birth. They told me we were eternal. With memorized words, I called to the lost and the damned. Come in: we are the ones who will never die.

We met behind the wall, he and I, and when our words ran dry, we put our hands upon our wicked bodies, kissed each other's wicked bellies and I found a home on his collarbone.

The ones who raised us had words for what we didn't want to be: lukewarm, lovers of the world. We wanted to be called righteous. Still we pressed into each other and prayed with hollow tongues.

2.

We were married inside the wall. Word by word we were bound: He and I and the blood and the body and we made our babies there, pouring holy water over their heads.

Now it is time to convince our lovelies that they need some kind of cosmic cleansing. That they are dirty and damned. We have reached the time to teach them the ways of salvation, of despising their flesh, their guts, their gardens. Give me the words for that.

Won't we teach them that their blissful baby bodies will blossom into something wrong and wanton? To view their wants as wicked? Won't we teach them that what the wall wants is something pure and faultless?

Inside the eyes of my daughters are galaxies of light, a kernel of a million exquisite lives. So what could I offer them when they came to me whole?

3.

He and I work our way to the edges, splintering with doubts in our Easter best. We found a door and the door was guarded. They warned we couldn't get back in but they cannot have our daughters, cannot shape them to be second and small and silent.

Sometimes I miss the feeling of being bounded in, the language of belonging, knowing which ground was mine to wander. Out here, everything is undefined and our old words leave us parched.

Now I wonder if we'll ever learn to feed our bodies what they crave, to value our own mirth and might, to sense our bodies prickle pull and not feel ashamed, to see every soul as a light and not a thing to save.

4.
I wonder how we lived before without music that floats in and through our skin like sugared light. There is more space here, more molecules to breathe and we even gasp now. We are delightfully ignorant, all the worlds a mystery and everyone in it. Who knows what magic we might make?

Outside the wall, we discover we might die. I've begun to believe I will truly cease. We feel the rush of death against the seconds of our lives and so we live them like twirling girls in dresses, just for the thrill of it.

We find new rituals, he and I. We wake most mornings to sounds of daughters rising. With sacred mouths, they are calling, "*We are open to miracles.*"

YOU WON'T DIE NOW. YOU WILL WATCH.

You won't die now

but you may suddenly lay upon the floor in the space behind the couch without warning, at times curled up, at times stretched out, unwilling to stand again for so long that each member of the family stops by to say a kind word or feed you a snack.

It's just one hole in the heart after another lately and where are we going anyway?

You have always had trouble moving forward when the destination is unclear. Remember the trip to New York City? And to Rome? Until you knew you were headed in the right direction, you were paralyzed mid-step while he motioned you forward saying *it's just around this corner.*

It's entirely unfair that your losses are minor and your coffee mug is deep with guilt. It's entirely unfair to try to make this mean something, to expect a destination and resolution and even repentance and and even peace. To expect things to come back. To expect not to suffer, even if your suffering is merely watching the world choke.

You won't die now. You will watch.

Because for us, it's a season of plenty, babies. We've got a house with a door and a lock where we wait out the cold and there's all the mango you could ask for. In the summer, as the virus digs into the lone star state, we land on unlimited screen time. We raise a herd of grazers who plow through loaves of bread, buckets of blueberries, peanut butter, raspberry jelly, and a small sea of iced water.

These are the gifts they set beside you on the floor in the space behind the couch saying *it's just around this corner, mama.*

DEAR MOM AND DAD

My mom and dad
Are living the same life
200 miles apart.

Apart for nearly all of my life,
they still do everything
at the same time.

They have grown old together
but I am the only one who knows.
They don't even realize it—the goofs.

Calling me minutes apart,
they tell me about their new air fryers,
their insulated coolers, the tests their docs are running.

They both ask me if I've ever tried toasted sesame oil.
Of course I have
because I am their daughter.

I have no memories
of us as a little trio,
of them as a match made in saltwater and salutes.

They split too soon
before our lives solidified
into stories stored on my mental map.

But now—straightened out a bit with age
freebirds with laugh lines,
I gather their parallel lives

and make them pose for pictures,
have them stand beside me on the occasions
when we are reunited. My halves.

Here's the confession:
I have been protecting my parents
from appearing here

because it's easier than saying
that somehow two things are true:
you did your best

except for when you didn't.
It hurt to be split in two
and I'm still waiting for an apology.

But, to my surprise, we all lived
long enough to be able to text each other
about eating Thai food, separately.

This wasn't the story
we wanted to write, was it?
But it got better about mid-way through.

SHUTDOWN LOVE SONG

Here is our window of time in which to be everything we ever wanted—
Unhurried, with our lives blending into each other.

All day, we are kneaded by three sets of hands, requests for toast and time
together. You have work to do. I had books to sell but now I am plaiting all our
separate pieces, an unending braid of every day's same to-do's. Didn't I once
want this? For work and rest and play to blend at the kitchen table with our
young ones running through our legs?

I just never imagined we'd do it alone.

At night in the quiet, we meet in the kitchen to race through limes, mint
leaves, sugar cubes and seasons of shows we missed in the before times when
we had meetings, openings, date nights. Before, when we could each take our
introverted hearts out alone sometimes for a solo espresso or a beer to hear our
own souls singing.

I didn't ask for it to come like this. I am twisted up in all the ways we are okay.

We have become a different pair these months.
You run yourself into a new body and I write myself a new soul.
Your hair grows long to your shoulders, mine to my waist.
You spend the morning on the sunny stone patio and I am in the garden.
I work on our soil, fill out the flower beds.
We find new places to be away
and we find new places to touch.
Funny how we've never grown tired of folding into each other, of taking turns
and taking care.

I call to my love, come, let's live under the live oaks and on Sunday nights, settle
into navy blue dust at dusk on our Gulf shores. Slip into seven o'clock ankle
waves and we will let our bedtime girls swing from our sandy arms and find
sun warmed places to tuck them in upon our chests.

POEM THAT RUNS THROUGH MY LIFE

The poem that runs through my life is a thirst to trek through time
to the places that don't know me, to meet the ones who I continue.

My blood is a braid that pulls me back to the lands where I am rooted.
Show me the soil that fed the stories that propagated into my prologues.

The poem that runs through my life is a homesickness
for where this olive skin is a sea, a native flower known along every path.

A part of me jostles in the back of a truck bed across Texas
up from the silver mines of Zacatecas.

A part of me trades Nordic snow for New York cement.

What wasn't in their bellies that they went hunting for?
What compels men to leave their mothers for America?

Help me understand—how did you brace for a homeless country
and a language without your name?

I wish to know where all these mothers in me are from.
And who packed all these poems? And mountain ranges.

I want to sing the song that's long lost behind my tongue
stunned, washed out, forgotten—what happened?

What dream was I? And whose?

To the ones who learned new words for me,
tell me, papas, how I'm doing. And how to cross borders.

HOUSEWIFERY AND POLITICS

When my mother-in-law comes over, I pick up the crap on the floor: wooden blocks, rubber bands, apple slices that have lost all resilience. I know I have nothing to prove. In fact, maybe I am proud.

The homes of all of the women in me are cluttered. My aunts, my granny, my mother: their tables are a maze of piled papers, plastic cartons of sliced cake, bowls of softening fruit, rubber bands, and the cords for things that are lost. My own countertops strewn with our things are my heritage.

They are also my rebellion. They say, I am a poet and I am not giving over my one beautiful life to be a stupid housewife. Although, I do... give my one life for this.

It's hard to value my work. Housewifery. The hours I spend tidying the counters and spraying them with vinegar or the never-ending bottle of Pinesol my mom bought me. My granny did this with five kids. My Mexican great-grandmother did it with fifteen. They called her Ma, rhymes with pie.

Sometimes I act like what they did was worthless. Like only the hands of my grandfathers did things worth wondering about.

She comes over tentatively, eager to see the girls but not as willing to answer my questions and look into my eyes. We disagree. What makes her feel safe threatens me and vice versa. She'll re-elect the President who calls Mexicans rapists as if his words didn't move that man from Dallas to get in his truck, drive to El Paso, and shoot at all the brown people in the Wal-Mart. He believed they could be rapists. And I believe they could be me.

It takes a great deal of effort. Just all of it. Being together. Puts her on edge. But she really needs to see my kids and feed them donuts so she bears it. She sits on my couch and I, for a second, relax and think of the kind of small talk my family works up in East Texas. Luckily, we both know the names of some plants and of course we both know her son and she can say "where is he" and I can say "on a run."

I wish I were on a run and not brooding over how to ask, "can you consider voting for someone who isn't trying to kill me?"

What is my history of reading poetry
Or what isn't my history of reading poetry
Or we marked every occasion with a poem
Or every poem was itself an occasion

No good thing in my life would exist
or at least they wouldn't exist quite the way they do
the way I like them to exist
without the poems we read
the poet names we traded
the phrases we shouted
the words I watched your lips curve around
the lines you put down into my ear.

TELL US ABOUT WHEN WE WERE LITTLE

I wonder what I will tell the girls about this year.

But also I'm afraid
what if they already know
—Then. In the future. What if they know then—
because every year after is like this, too.

A mad parade of state violence and mass migration, an entire state engulfed in fire, a pandemic, the loony applause of a fascist cult, unemployment lines, food lines, lines to vote, and so many lines to say this isn't happening, that you can't believe what you see, plus the hurricane, and how our neighbor Doug said it's the worst year of his life because he lost his job after 25 years when the pandemic shut down the state and the company he sold seafood for shutdown for keeps.

I am afraid it isn't dramatic anymore to wonder
what if the really crazy times that I'll tell them about
are the before times.

I'll say
it used to rain more.
We used to touch.

Our world is always ending.

IT'S A CLASSIC WILL THEY OR WON'T THEY

Sometimes you will wonder if it's time to buy a gun. It will feel like everyone is arming up. In fact, the newspaper says so. More Americans bought their first gun this summer than any time ever before. They say, give me whatever you've got. The shelves are empty.

Sometimes you will wonder if you are being naive. If the division will really spill out onto the streets. And not just the streets downtown and at the Capitol but your street. The street where you walk barefoot in the mornings in your robe while your kid spots sand and school buses. You will wonder if they will come for you because you are weak, because you didn't load up. Because you put out a flag that says I'm easy and my love is free.

Sometimes you will fall asleep afraid. You will look out the window from your bed with the quilt across your sweaty body at the silhouettes of trees swaying against the city-lit sky and you will wonder how long it will be until they come for you.

You will wonder what is the easiest way to disappear or if you have it in you to fight and how did it come to this.

RADICAL TENDERNESS // THE GAME

When I was six, I pretended to be God and I made so many flowers. Everywhere I looked, out popped tiny flowers. Daisies, wildflowers, those little white onion flowers. I felt happy and powerful.

Soon after, I was sitting in a tree with my cousin and I said we should play this game but she made a face and said it was bad to pretend to be God. So I never imagined that again.

I heard someone ask on the radio, "if you could choose, what would you want heaven to be like?" It reminded me of the game and now that I'm older and more free, I'm ready to play again.

If I were the Creator, I would start with the flowers. Wildflowers everywhere. And also peonies, ranunculus, hibiscus, althea, star jasmine, marigolds. So many marigolds and the David Austin roses my friend Anna cuts out of magazines and sends in the mail all the way from Buffalo.

I would bring back the animals and bugs. All the ones we've lost. Beavers, wolves, and all the birds. The nightingales and monarchs. Lasso the carbon from the sky and tuck it back into the soil. I could clean up the oceans but they wouldn't stay that way. You have to get to the thing under the thing, the cause: it's the humans. Humans, with their big hair and dancing butts and funny stories.

I would keep making them the same way: out of stardust, explosions of planets and moons, from ancient grains of volcanic dust and history, despite their tendency to fall into chasms of fear, to leap violently into visions of righteousness. Although they convince themselves that there is never enough which makes them freak out and take everything, if I tweaked everything at once, the Earth might shoot straight into the Sun like a pin ball.

But here's what I would change that might help them stop hoarding everything, stop plunking all their old mattresses into the ocean. When they came to the end—however it happened—lungs filled with fluid, a foreign object lodged into their soft bodies, the multiplication of cells—however it happened, when they reached the end, I would bring them to a new beginning.

I know—you've heard of that. It's not original but here's what I want to try. What if each time they start over, it's better? More tender.

No matter what. For everyone. You've probably already figured out that there's no lake of fire, no hell except for our present violence. Hunger and disease. The genocides, and worse—pretending the genocides didn't happen. The enslavement of everyone everywhere by people who now pretend they had nothing to do with that, who now pretend it isn't what messed everything up. Plus, private prisons and war in general.

Anyway—no additional hell. And no punishment. At least, not from me. They can keep grappling with whatever accountability means and I hope they get that right.

I want to try radical tenderness. No questions asked. Whenever they emerge into the next place, I wanna make it beautiful. Even for the worst ones, the ones who have eaten our hearts and brains.

When they wake up, I'm giving them a Papa who loves to cook breakfast. Eggs, bacon, cinnamon toast. He'll already have a jar filled with cinnamon and sugar for dusting the buttered bread.

He won't ask about all that stuff before. He doesn't know about it. Clean slate. They mostly don't either although a feeling of shame may ping inside from time to time. They might stare across a field at dusk filled with fireflies and wonder— who could ever deserve a life so good?

I won't make demands—like about saving the world or curing this or that. There's no debt to pay. New system: radical tenderness. I'm going to put some good books on the shelves and music in their ears. I'm giving them friends who teach them to shout lines of poetry into the wind in the places where gravel roads end.

I'll let someone good show up for them at the right time. Someone with a flute of a voice and an ocean inside.

And if they get married, that Papa I gave them? He'll collect the flowers from outside the church and plant them in his own garden. He'll save the seeds every spring and watch them grow again. Each year, he'll offer them the seedlings of the wedding flower. No matter what. Even if they didn't call as much. Even if they let the last sprouts sit too long in the sun and they crumpled up. It's unconditional. Wedding flowers every year.

We'll just see what happens. It's going to take time to make a dent but we have time. At least I do, in the game. They'll keep closing their eyes. And waking up to a table set just for them. To a surprise September cool front. To a card filled with cut-outs of David Austin roses, just because.

TENTH ANNIVERSARY SENTIMENTAL

It was just as hot as ten summers ago, as hot as when we danced with our friends in the courtyard with suit jackets, ties, shoes sweat through, shucked, and piled to the side.

The night before, we stayed up late. We noticed it was midnight as we fell into bed so we leapt to our knees and bounced around on the mattress. Our cheers were hushed so we wouldn't wake anyone.

Happy Anniversary!
Ten years!
Sign me up for ten more!

In the morning, he made the coffee like he was singing our favorite song. *Today is the birthday of our family. Today we are a celebration.* He wore a gray button-up and I chose my champagne dress. The girls wore dresses but no shoes. Pink tulle. Navy blue velveteen. And white lace.

When we first said hello, when we drove those hours back and forth, when we read poems to each other line by line—how could we have known—that there would be a garden where we would cross the crushed gravel with bare feet to an altar of milkweed with three little dreamers and a priest and we would promise: another ten.

What we didn't say: *you are not the same one as before.*
What we felt: *I will share my cup with you every day and every night for as long as you want.*
What we did after: jump on the trampoline.

In the last hours, we found our way back to the kitchen table. We ate a never-ending meal, Chef Jane's heart-filled food: roasted chicken on fragrant rice, a salad of every herb and pickled pepper, crisped potato, the best hummus of our life, smokey vegetable kebabs, and a strawberry chocolate pie, the crust flaked with butter and salt, topped with six inches of cream, a spectacle of fushia flowers and a chocolate hooray.

AS IF ASKED HOW TO KEEP THE LIGHT ON

People ask me how to be a parent and an artist. Here is the secret. When you think, "If I do not take a walk outside in the rain right now, I will die. The last remaining flicker of light will go dark," you take yourself seriously. You do whatever it takes to walk in the rain. You listen. You jot things down while people pass you by and all they think is that idiot can't get off her phone long enough to take a walk but what is really true is that you are trying to keep from extinguishing.

THE BON BONS ARE YOUR BIRTH RIGHT

Let's drop all those jokes about bon bons
because this is something real I do
caretaking or living or making things
and what you are doing—it is not nothing.

Listen, we are not machines or at least we don't have to be
because we all deserve rest and pleasure
and we don't have to earn it.
Our labor isn't what gives us the right to live.

Who said you could water the plants
for hours in your silk robe and smoke

And by what right do you sit down with a mug and stare past the sky?
By what right do you sit still to let the cat nap on your lap?
By what right do you take a day, or two days, to let grief demolish you?
By what right do you ride around with music so loud,
those old songs from college that put a stupid smile on your face
and you laugh at how making out
could last for hours when you were 19?
By what right do you set the table with candles just for you
and who told you that you could gather your sons
and eat lobster on New Years with butter dripping down your chin?

Did you pay off all that debt yet?
Did you cross every item off your list?
Did you clock in and out, max out that overtime?
Did you do it all and do it all and do it all and do it all again to the letter?

The bon bons are your birth right
your I'm-a-human-being right
your seeing and smelling and tasting and hearing and touching,
oh yes, and touching rights
and maybe you don't have all five of those
and maybe you do but you can't feel them anymore

but what on earth are we doing here
if not staring googley-eyed at whatever is bursting to life
at whatever still spins on this spinning marble
at whatever we have not yet killed and quantified?

A WASTE

If I spend the day sprawled out in the grass fanned by the leaves and September breeze and if all I name today are cloud shapes and all I sock away is sunshine into young temporal lobes, have I become less valuable, have I become a waste? And when I have ceased to do this beautifully and with a pleasant sound, who will throw me out onto the burn pile?

AS IF ONE HAD THE RIGHT TO COMPLAIN

The pandemic is making women quit their jobs and it is no different for me. This year I was supposed to be wearing my author hat, my Story Time Lady hat. This year I was supposed to be able to buy a hat with money I earned from the fantastic picture book I wrote and published while pregnant last year.

But I can't do that now. Because we can't gather into a circle and listen to a story and scrounge around in the same box of pastels and make things together.

So I am supposed to switch gears and "still be a writer." This is what my friends told me when I tried to tell them how much it sucked that my business imploded. When I said I was struggling they reasonably replied, "Well you can still write, right?"

It feels impossible to explain why this is not possible, why the men in my writers group are working on novels and nearing 50,000 words and completing multiple screenplays while I am scrapping together poems.

Here are the conditions under which you must create phenomenal art:

after nights of no sleep with a teething baby who alternates between crying and sitting on my head, after everyone has been fed and the clutter chaos has been reduced marginally, after the baby has been put down for a nap, after paper and markers have been fetched, after pee has been wiped from the floor, after the groceries have been listed and purchased and washed and put away and even prepped for consumption, with a pot of soup on, with children racing by, with children leaping over the furniture, with children climbing the counters, with children running into the dog's water bowl every single day, with whirling and colliding, with the volume too high, with their manic bursts of energy, with their tender spirits, with their needs for touch and soft voices, with some sense of responsibility to be kind to them, to read to them and be altogether lovely to them, after making significant amounts of eye contact, while facilitating some sense of wonder and playfulness and freedom and adventure, while trying not to cave to your shittiest impulses, while doing everything you can not to yell so loud the doors fall off their hinges, and without pay, without benefits, without healthcare, knowing that your retirement relies entirely on the generosity of your partner, without respect, without empathy for what you are tasked with or what you actually accomplish, while shouldering the blame for choosing this, while shouldering how pathetic it is that you love this more than paychecks, while wanting a fucking paycheck, while running a marathon through each day and night that looks like a big blank gap on your resume, while dreading what would happen if your plans and safety nets just poof! disappeared! and you look like a joke trying to get a sub job or a job as a barista twenty years too late, also while knowing that no one wants to read the complaints of a mom, of a Mooommmm, of a mom mom mom mom mom mom mom mom mom mom.

And my mom, who has always worked more than one job cannot entertain that this struggle is real. She just looks at me with disgust and says how many women would kill to do this, as if one had the right to complain.

Under these conditions, write a poem.

Maybe it is just the shitty sleep. Yesterday, I kid you not, I wrote, "And this is rose-colored nothing: some mornings I begin by nursing my baby who has slept through the night and her two sisters crowd in under my wings and rest their bed rumpled heads on her and I think I am so happy and I am so happy."

Maybe with the right amount of sleep it doesn't seem like an exhausting amount of work.

Maybe with the right amount of sleep it seems like I am actually making something beautiful and the mess is charming and the noise is charming and the brain fog is charming and relying on my partner is charming and that these staccato moments between housewifery and writers block are actually something that one could call a creative practice.

AS IF ASKED WHO I'M WRITING FOR

"It is important to know who
You want to be proud of you."
—Nikki Giovanni

My oldest daughter is sitting at the dining room table. She was packed for a sleepover at her grandmother's house, strapped into her seat in the car, and then with no warning began crying and begging to stay home so she could make cozy nests and draw. I drove her sisters across town and came home to make poems in the quiet. And now she is at the table. She is drawing with markers on a hand-stapled book of blue paper. She is writing a story in pictures. The story is about a girl who wakes up secretly every morning to see the sun rise.

All I've got from my great grandfather Gustavo are the same stories of him crossing into Texas on foot and working decades at the sawmill until one of his last living daughters unearths a new story. Joey says he always smelled of sawdust, that he would let her sit on his lap, pour his coffee into a saucer for her. She remembers him reading his mataburros, his dictionary and encyclopedias. At night his children would follow him into the yard to look at the stars, themselves a constellation. We were always a long way from ever meeting but in his only color photograph, I spy my long nose like an arrow.

When Granny was young she liked to climb trees and she wore her dark hair short. When she fell in love she got married in secret and spent the night dancing with her new family. She has always found a way to slip me snacks, lipstick, and gold earrings.

In the seventh grade I tricked my only Hindu friend into coming to church with me so that she could get saved. A woman I trusted told my friend that everyone in India would go to hell. When we grew up, the memory burned me alive. I apologized and she told me that foul night pushed her to learn about her own faith and I say that is the only good thing that could have happened. She emails to say she has sent my picture books to every nephew and this is who I want to be proud of me.

AS IN, I'VE HELD BLIZZARDS UPSIDE DOWN

Dairy Queen now has dairy-free Dilly Bars!
This is cause for celebration because I eat very little dairy now. The special Dilly Bars are made with coconut cream.

Every time we go to DQ I have to remind my daughters or the person handing me a dilly bar that my first job was at Dairy Queen so they know I know what it's like to turn the blizzards upside down, not to mention how to lug the boxes of sweet milk from the freezer to pour down the gullet of the blizzard machine.

This boy I liked, Leo, helped get me the job. Our boss Stefani was a thirty-something white woman who said if you have time to lean, you have time to clean. One time I took a cleaning rag and started cleaning the grubby broom handle.

With my hand around the broom handle, I wiped up and down with firm strokes to get all the grime off.

When I looked up, all of my co-workers, who were all kids from my high school and Mexican moms, were frozen, staring at me. Then they all burst into hysterical laughter. Even Leo. He looked embarrassed to love me.

In school I was really smart, but at DQ I was dumber than dumb. They barely trusted me to make toast. They seemed very concerned I would lock myself in the freezer on accident. When it was my job to mop the floor, I mixed toxic chemicals that gave everyone a headache.

We had to tuck extra-large polo shirts into waist-high black pants and walk drive-through orders out to people's cars behind the building and I always wanted to cover my butt with the tray or something when I was walking away because I could feel people staring. And we had to wear visors. I shit you not. For minimum wage.

So yeah, I'm going to keep squeezing every last ounce of credit out of my time at Dairy Queen.

AS IF THE SUMMER WOULD NEVER END

1.
In the rage of the heat of the summer
when the sun seems to sit upon our chests
the leaves and the petals of every plant across the garden
give up for good or for a spell turn yellow.

There is a part of me now, especially now,
when secret police patrol and scientific information goes missing,
that doesn't believe anything good is coming,
that doesn't want to know what's coming next,
that would prefer to sleep through it.

I am, in these days, the slanted peak
of a dying tree, broken off at the face
an insolent wound
a cautionary tale of the chance of lightning
or the power of decay
the decay of hope
the birth of cynicism.

Yet anyone who has dug hands into the light softness of a dead tree
felt surprised at its raspy sound and easy tear
has uncovered many minute practitioners of resurrection
as the poet farmer says
to be a cynic is to be dead
but even decaying trees are grounds for regeneration.

A hope blows in, a zillion hopes burrow down below
passing through one microbe to the next and the next
pulling the weight of doom down to be digested and made new.

2.
As the dog days wind down,
we chance at cool mornings—indeed we delight as
the sigh of a storm in the Gulf gives some relief

from 100 degree afternoons
though we know it whirls destruction on unluckier coasts.

We are reminded of what we know comes next
of what is certain, we are
relieved that what feels permanent now will pass away.

On these days, when the leaves breathe relief and shudder,
when stalk and vine and branch perceptibly perk up
despite being heat-beaten for months and parched
knowing full well in their roots that summer and her torments
will continue after this freak cool spell burns up the dry air.
The petals nearly prance and sun-sugared fruits plump up.

In this brief reprieve, knowing somewhere in my blood and bones
what is still happening on the street, I am overpowered by a small peace
and the only paradox I'll admit to knowing—
that we can still feel good when things are bad.

Don't think I get it just because I said it.
It's just that even when our reality shut down,
when every door closed and we realized our neighbors
would hoard toilet paper in the back of their vans,
would take name calling to the next level—to vilification, criminalization
would lust over locking us up, would even count on a strange prophecy of
beheading the other
even then, we were still happy a time or two a day
perhaps three times at the table
or once in the bed in the last minutes of another scorched night.

3.
There are millions of us afraid and fleetingly glad
Millions of us who march and resist, shuffle and slide
scoot booties across the dance circles that break out in the middle of a march.
We are blooming through the asphalt cracks
and sprouting up like laughs across the ash-strewn forest floor.

On those paradox days when we preview autumn's relief
we sprawl across the lawn under a hint of rain with the dry air floating in,
and I think I might be the purple flowers
that open every morning, persistent dreamers
who fall on the ground at dusk when the mosquitos swarm
and then at sunrise are reborn.

Or perhaps I am the profound faith of fern fronds
sprouting from a fallen tree
laid out across a green gold pond

In the nub of the tree's broken branch,
there am I—waving fresh spouts of something new.

PART III

PANDEMIC FALL

AS IN, HOW ARE YOU GOING TO LEAVE WHEN THEY'RE STILL HERE

We have declared today "Fall Day" in Houston. It is the day the mosquitos skip town and the first day we think sweaters and pumpkin. I will admit that I am thinking pumpkin. I am thinking muffins and pancakes and maple syrup and salted butter. And when evening comes early, I am thinking of roasting root vegetables, eating them atop fettuccine with goat cheese and kale crisped under oil, heat, and salt. I am thinking of socks and leather shoes and October birthdays. I am thinking of how to stay warm and how to delight in dry air and open windows.

I admit to you that in the climax of the summer I studied ways to move to Canada. I thought we have got to get out of here. I thought one day they'll kill us if we don't. They will foof out our light unless we buy guns and join them in their war. That is summer's climax. That is finally feeling dis-enfranchised and powerless. That is a new feeling to me. Imagine waking up in a world where you can be killed in your own home and the only one who gets an apology is your neighbors. Imagine generations of doing right and having a voice that never tires of falling on deaf ears. We cannot leave. We cannot leave. We cannot because this is exactly what people do—rush to the center of the raft. We push everyone out of the way to get to safety. Whatever we have to do to forget that the struggle worked for us until the struggle came for us, too.

And that is why I think yes, pumpkin. We will need muffins and pie. We will need corn with butter and the alchemy of caramel and pecans. We will dig joy out of the ground and we will gather it from the trees. We will milk it, churn it, and knead it. We will let it set or let it brown or let it smoke or let it rise. We will set the table with joy and arrange bouquets of joy that spill over. We will carry out platters so heavy with joy that it strains our arms and place joy in front of our beloveds and slather joy over our thick slices of bread. We will drizzle it and dollop it. We do whatever we must do to sustain and we stay and we repair and repay, linking arms on fall days, stirring up a ceaseless chant demanding: liberation. For everyone.

SEPTEMBER 29 WISHLIST

Convert the endless summer into something I can slip through my lips and pop with a violent splash of guts against my tongue. I would like you to make for me a tomato.

MILK AND FLOWERS

The children want to play with me, want me upside down on the climbing dome, want me walking the slackline one bare foot in front of the other, with them bouncing, laughing, their long hair trembling behind them like wind chimes. The children want to spin elegant scripts and cast me as the mother always, want me to follow them into the make believe rain and scoop them up and cook them make believe soups and cakes under a tent of our old quilts. And I will consent to play until I can no longer leave the books of poems unread and the lines about milk and flowers unwritten and the pot of potato soup on the real stove unstirred. And that is when true play begins, when I am extracted and all ties to the real real unravel and their stories manifest across the confines of walls and what their mother is able to pretend. Or believe. Same word.

AS IF I HAD MY OWN PLAN, AS IF I HAD NOT COME TO GET PREGNANT

When in Venice, you will behave like a tourist no matter how many times you scoff at the ones fresh off the cruise ships, the ones taking pictures of themselves in gondolas and eating pizza ordered from plastic sheathed menus along the canal dripping grease onto the red and white checkered tablecloths.

No matter how many lines I drew between myself and them, I was still them seven years ago when I ordered cappuccino in the afternoon.

Here we go, they thought, another American drinking milk after lunch and I thought I know I know I know but I am an American.

I have come to your old and beautiful country to make love every evening with my young husband and to eat gelato after dinner and buy a copy of my favorite book in a language I do not speak.

I have come to feel small and young, speck-like and satiated, to marvel at how many miles I can walk down cobblestone streets and how much I can eat and drink.

I have come to marvel at myself just as much as the statues, the paintings, the Venetian architecture, the lore, the time we walked up to a small archway where a mezzo soprano was singing Ave Maria.

To marvel at the way the sun shines into green tomatoes here, turns them into ruby pops of sun-burned sugar.

To marvel at my own hunger for crawling into another body when an afternoon cappuccino heads off any desire for a nap.

My, my, and what a bruised tomato I was when one of my companions asked me, as we sprawled across the sidewalk near a canal, sated with Campari sodas and crostinis, *but what do you want to do with your life?*

And after stammering that up until now I had only thought of setting up my husband's life, I realized I did not know.

PEOPLE KEEP KNOCKING ON MY DOOR TO LECTURE ME

The man whose fleet of employees care sometimes for our yard knocked on my door after seven months to tell me my husband didn't cut the grass enough and didn't I want my house to look nice and that the HOA would come slap a fine on my door if I didn't let him cut my grass, mulch the garden beds, clean off the roof, and repair the fence. He knows how easily my arm is twisted but what he doesn't know is how many poems I have written about the yard and the garden and that my favorite descriptors are wild and rambling. He knows the fence must be replaced but what he doesn't know is how my belly turned to lava the last time he was here when he walked by me and kissed my cheek without a word, actually with a smile. And that day I was speechless. So today, when I told him my girls think the weeds are pretty and that all I had money for was their birthday presents and that talking shit about my favorite person was not a great way to get me to spend money, he relented and left me to my beautiful squalor.

The next day, a woman knocked on my door with my own dog on a leash. When I opened the door to let my dog in she stepped inside my home without an invitation and without a mask. I thanked her for bringing my dog and waited for her to leave. But she kept coming up with reasons to make me repent. *He came into my house! I've seen him through the hole in your fence! He's been gone for hours! He needs to wear a collar if you're going to let him get out.* She kept adding points to her sermon to find a way to bring me to my knees. And sure, I deserved a scolding but who is suffering? This beast of a dog who got to run and play with other dogs for the first time in seven months? Who has been sleeping in a leather club chair for nine years? This dog with a big backyard and five humans who give him pats and scratches and lumps of cheese?

Please lady, next time tell me what you want and speak plainly. And you, sir, say it. You want money. You want work. You want my elaborate gratitude. Say it. Say you want me to feel the deficiencies of my love.

AS IN, DEACTIVATE

What if this is it? And there is nothing after? And we are all just here and then we are not?

What if heaven was always just a word describing the height of joy which always shows up with her twin—the desire to make this feeling last forever?

But it is fleeting and so are we.

Am I content to live half-alive, filtering my touch, taste, smell, hearing through sight? Through what can be seen and shared with a general audience?

I want to write letters that say Dear You and Only You

I want to taste salt and fat, let it dance across my mouth from wall to tongue, and not share the scene from above in a square with whoever has a feeling they can't bear, with whoever comes scrolling by.

I want to let unexpected hawk cries in the afternoon, midnight hoots and screeches, warbling coos and calls catch me off guard.

I desire to sing Happy Birthday to a girl in a blue dress on her sixth anniversary of being alive without our song being snared in a file to sock away and relive without first being fully lived, without first viewing her through a screen that is too small to show me the pine green flecks of soul in her emerald eyes.

How could living fast and only half-embodied ever fill our well with what is real—with the soft shock of petals, with the crunch of snow or carrots chopped for soup, with the ache in our gut muscles after a hard laugh or loss? Fill me up or not at all! I want the real deal of living, as excruciating and boring and deadly as it may be. Rouse me. Even if it is just for this one small life.

I want to be here if this is it.

And if it's not? Surprise me.

ALL THIS TIME HER BONES

Have you come to the part of your life in which you contemplate your mother's bones? Have you thought about her blood, about the fine material wrapped around her precious nerves, the delicate routes of communication down her spine, down her sturdy legs? Have you reached the place in your life in which you feel the pain in your mother's feet? Do the pinpricks in her toes which she hardly minds at all keep you up at night? What is this place, this unexpected mile marker, newly erected monument invisibly constructed, this life landmark commissioned on the unwelcome occasion when I begin to study my mother's movements, begin to watch for signs of slowing, startling shutters, or symptoms of hyphenated conditions, begin looking back at our shared youth, begin looking forward dimly. I remember everything. I am the repository of her youth. All this time her bones, and blood, and nerves have been mattering to me in the way the ground matters, is matter, matters so much that it disappears until I notice first signs of erosion, until I notice newly uneven crags, paths that trail off, tremors, first signs of cracks and all of a sudden the ground is showing up, snagging my attention and I am looking down at it in a new way. I am wondering how many more of my footfalls it will catch, how much longer it will hold me.

LATE OCTOBER ROAD TRIP, THE ELECTION HAS BEGUN

1.

We wave goodbye to our house, our fortress, our forest, our garden, our office, our cafe, our everything for the past eight months heading north on a Friday afternoon for the purpose of stepping into someone else's bubble, to sprawl on their couches and peer through the blue light of their refrigerator, to inspect their flowers and books and Netflix queues. We begin with children's songs and Clementine laughs through every line of There's A Hole in My Bucket. We take the interstate north from the pines to the prairies. I-45 and I-35 have run through our years like the spines of novellas. Now it is always I-45, Houston to Dallas.

II.

I used to love to road trip alone. Now there are five of us in the car, fries in between the seats and two unsweet teas. Have you ever traveled with three small children? Does the thought flip you upside down? It's neither easy nor difficult, just a lot of planning, adapting, and saying yes to milkshakes, potty breaks, and answering life's burning questions like what do squirrels eat and what do cows eat and what do skunks eat and why won't the president's wife make him be good. The six-year old turns introspective and silent in the far back seat as she always does in the car. The baby sleeps. I drive and all I ask for is cruise control and endless podcasts. He scrolls and talks to me. People passing us make hand gestures, sometimes thumbs up but usually not. I think it is the bumper stickers. We drive north without stops for as long as our bladders hold.

III.

We've become practiced, too, at holding our breath every time we pass painted red signs, ominous flags, and billboards with cult favorite 45 haunting and taunting like a wound that never stops bleeding. He is our wound, our favorite way of getting all wound up. And yes, I said our favorite. Yes, I have come to believe we mistake outrage for action. It feels like we are doing something when it does something to us. In the garden, I adore unearthing a grub worm fat on the juicy roots of my plants. What is disgust if not delight to flip something onto a brick and smash it with the back of a spade, a juicy pus explosion? At least with the worms I am moved to action. I have quit clicking on anything that says his name because this pain is unavoidable, it is viral, hovering in every direction on every thoroughfare. I am doing my best not to nurse this wound but to heal it with laughter and action and paying attention to trees. I name the trees along the highway: sweetgum, water oak, black tupelo, loblolly pine, and elm. Finally, we come to a doorway through which we can walk and exhale: watching our risk, worries, and thrill dance through the particulate air. We hesitate and do we dare? We hug. This is what we came for.

IV.

We begin by staring at each other's children. When they laugh, we laugh. When they cry, we act hurt. When they argue, I say "they will work it out. Let's have wine." "Which kind?" "Your best." We find our way around asking how are you doing and where have you been and not been, who have you not seen, what haven't you watched, which books have you started, how do you fall asleep. We don't ask what do you think will happen, who do you think will win, when will we see you again. No one knows anything. We say, "we are doing okay" because we have learned not to confuse empathy for the oppressed with actually being oppressed ourselves.

V.

I hug my niece for the first time since the last time it was cold. Since before. And my daughters make her laugh. I sit at the table with her mothers and they tell me what it's like to travel through the South ready to say they are sisters. And I have heard what it is like to drive down a country road with trucks parked bumper to bumper in the ditches, neighbors waving red flags and screaming at cars as if it is a crime just to be alive and not on their side. Tonight at the table, all I can say to their faces is I am going to do something about it. I cannot keep saying that the state of things is crazy because it's not—it's just true.

VI.

At night I lay in the dark on a trundle bed and watch videos on my phone until I realize I don't disagree with any of them and this becomes so eerie that I put it down and stare at a balloon bobbing along the ceiling until the baby wakes for milk.

VII.

It's an intimacy to wear tired pajamas around people you haven't sworn your life to. It's Saturday. No one slept and we fill our mugs to the brim with black coffee. Clementine plays race cars with her cousin over and over. Anabelle is out of her mind and runs the babies around the kitchen and down the hall.

Being with people is a funny drug. I wonder what it is we are doing here over barbecue and pumpkin beers with the kids clomping up the stairs? What was worth the risk of travel during a pandemic? Whatever it is, I think it is a healing thing, worth the sunken gut feeling we got every time we passed those signs pocking Texas, our Texas—where the settlers have never stopped fearing that their land would be taken back by the people from whom they took it and from the people who worked it and work it and work it. Lately, I've been saying we're doing okay, because who would not break eye contact if I confessed that life is suffering and if not, it's a struggle to make it less painful for others. And lately, I've been calling myself a caregiver because there's no space to say what is a mother if not someone who shows a child how to not look away. What does Marge Piercey say about pain? "At first you can stare at it. Then it blinds you." So maybe what we are doing here is resting our eyes.

VIII.
On Sunday we go hurtling home on the side of the highway that would spit us into the Gulf of Mexico if we closed our eyes and flew past our shady bungalow that waits for us behind the gun shop. Anyone who has driven through the Lone Star State knows that the feeders are full of fried chicken, truck stops, Czech pastries, dusty little churches with gravel parking lots, and miles of ranch land lined with white metal fence and barbed wire. In the ditches, there are crosses and fabric bouquets, a roofer's ladder, shredded tires and skunks, bits of beasts disregarded by the vultures, billboards with quotes attributed to God, and demands for women to "choose life" which always makes me wonder why my twenty-two year old mother did and if she would ever tell me how close we came to this reality just not existing. Southbound, we five are cocooned in soothing podcast voices and plans that reach far past our destination, plans to vacate one of these days. The girls they say they want to go to Paris, they want to go some place where it snows, sell their stuffed animals and live in a school bus that can fly. Lately, I've been saying we're doing okay because who has time for a treatise on weekend diversions during a pandemic, because who wants to hear that we're always home, no matter what happens, no matter where we go.

HOPE, A PRACTICE

Hope counts on tomorrow no matter how unlikely tomorrow might be. Hope says there's a chance so we should plant the tomatoes, water them every day. The planet is warming and it doesn't come down to us really the way it comes down to the factories, captains of industry, alliances and general interest. But hope plants a tree in the front yard anyway because there is a chance that in other weedy yards and forests of ash and char, someone else could be untangling tender roots, lowering thirsty tendrils into damp black soil alive with possibilities.

COMING TO TAKE IT

There are 18 days until the election and is it confidence
throttling the drumbeat thrum of my blood?
We could still lose and then we could still really lose
but there are teens organizing their first marches
and that guy who rolled up next to me
and pumped his first at my bumper sticker.

These are things you hope you can hope upon.
Plus, the long lines to vote now stretch for miles and hours
full of fanatics and those who are jumping ship
and all of us guessing at what this might mean.

In the first days of early voting I take one daughter
and we dress in team colors.
We walk past the community center
where we always vote, along the line of neighbors
with their eyes reading us and our eyes reading them.

We pass the library, the park, walk all the way
to the concert hall—the end of the line.
I take my place and try to interpret tribal alliances
from the backs of heads. This tick, looking
to hats and car bumpers and front yards
for signs of allegiance, I resent this part of myself.

A man hands out "official voter guides"
with red checkmarks for patriotism
and I put up my hand to say no.

My daughter, who always mixes up the names
of the president and his challenger,
gathers acorns in the shade
and the line moves forward.

There are red flags draped across the bike rack,
red flags draped across the bus stop.
There are red signs lined up edge to edge,
tiny walls creating uncrossable borders.

We shuffle and listen for code words
collect acorns, this is our line life.

Up front by the community center doors,
a truck is stretched across two spaces
flying a loyal flag and another that taunts
"come and take it."

And I think I am
coming to take it.

Near the door, two men in blue jeans and caps
trade stories about their rallies
about their peak spiritual experiences.
Best nights of their lives, they say.
They went home glowing like
radioactive mushrooms.

We, the collective line,
breathe slow and shallow behind our masks
and I try to look past the loons.

Where is the anxiety? The despair.
I thought I'd be more riled up but somehow
that dial has been turned down in me.

Lately, our life is a series of Sundays.
We take walks through mid-October humidity
as thick as pumpkins
and we smile like jack-o-lanterns
when the girls make us laugh
with their little booty dances
and their tangoes of language.

I have stopped all scrolling
of any kind, stopped
reading what is recommended, stopped
letting algorithmic waves carry me out
to where I cannot swim, cannot stay afloat
in bottomless seas of outrage.

It is enough to tend to the wells of sadness
my little loves dangle above
when they think of everyone they used to know.

It is nearly my turn and I know
which boxes I will check and I know
I will not sleep on November 3 and I know
I cannot feel as disappointed as four years ago
when I was a child and since then
all of my childhood heroes have been unmasked.
Who they are and what they'll do
to manifest destiny cannot come
as a surprise anymore.

They say it may last a week, a month.
They say it may last and it may last and it may last.

If I were a cynic, would I be in line with my daughter
now flashing my I.D., now squaring up to the machine.
Would I keep trying to filter honey-hued days
and our daily dose of terror into poems?

Do all cynics claim to still feel
the warmth of some light? That is,
if I had lost the light, would I even know it?
Could I mistake it for that radioactive rally glow?

There are darker places we could fall.
But brighter, too,
so all we can do is march into the booth
or across the bridge or around and around
the halls of power
to do the best we can with whatever light we have
or can recall, each one of us
suited in red and blue and bruised
and masked in fear and guilt and possibly, a hope
for a world in which we can all
breathe easy again or
for once.

NOVEMBER 2, 2020

Before
Before election day
Before the last of these voting lines and polls
Before we know
Before anyone's disappointment

We wait
Practicing patience
While we manage dread
While we can make calls, text, knock on doors
While predictions are made and bets are placed
We shuffle around shuttering and shrugging because

Tomorrow
Tomorrow we may not know
Tomorrow is the last day to do anything about it
Tomorrow we make no themed snacks
Tomorrow we leave the champagne to chill at the grocery store
Tomorrow I will wrestle my daughters, hold them, walk with them down golden leaf pathways as far as they will go, tuck them into bed. I will lay beside them long past the quiet moment when they fall gently into rest.

On election night, I know a woman who will meet with her friends for a virtual joy fest. They will clink drinks through the screen, extolling the year's joys and unexpected wins. They will save the news for tomorrow. And I think she is wise.

Between now and knowing, I will buy plants, hunt for sun patches in the yard to break into, hack away at old roots, dig until I get deep, past the dark dirt on the surface, into the copper colored clay and tawny sand that has been here all this time. Maybe—
I'll plant a tree.

CERTITUDES, NOVEMBER 4

As gloved hands count votes I think
do Black women expect to feel
disappointed every two years
and they still show up—

I wish I wrote words better
words that rise to the occasion.

I have a friend
whose father and grandmother died last year.
2020 was supposed to be her year
but then of course it wasn't.

Her mother just received a diagnosis
and my friend said it best:
once you accept
that someone is dying,
it's easier watching them go.

On the dark night in 2016,
Clementine was a week old
I nursed her in the light
of an electoral map nightmare
and fell asleep afraid.

Now she is four.

What are we going to do, if—
We will get her to eight.
We will get the baby to 5.
And Anabelle to 10.

That's all I can predict tonight.

ON THE AFTERNOON OF NOVEMBER 6

Saturday.
What jubilation is this—
A fiesta of peace
A mouthful of hope
A tango with stupid joy
Merriment

We are wild dancers in the front yard whooping.
We are loud and slobbery video calling all our friends to pump fists.

Sunset is soft dripping hot gold down the face of every leaf.
I bike fast around the neighborhood
with a funny face laughing.
Am I in love again—

"RESISTANCE IS FERTILE"

Four years ago I marched
behind a sign that said "resistance is fertile."
Now, here we are.

Artists of the resistance,
this is your moment
to take a heap of honey,
a holy moon-glow dollop
to scoop it up and press it
between your brows
a loving smush
an anointment
and break into whole body harmony
gospel level vibrato, all of you.

Because of what you brought to canvas
what you found the words for
what beats you let stream
what you did to say "we are still here"
what you did to uproot, bridge over, and put down
certainly cracked open some places that needed cracking open
certainly let in the light.

Did you slog through, artists?
Did you want to quit and did you not?

And if you did
didn't you come back?

And if you stopped to rest
and never again crawled out of bed
you can bet we made extra
to cover you.

The gifts you gave in dissonance, in fury,
thick in black ink, the yarns you spun
in tension and release

the foundations you ground up
pounded into a chalky paint
swirled into the reworking of an old story, certainly

retooled what was broken, certainly
gave someone words to say "I am still here."

THE ERRAND

I took Clementine out today to exchange her birthday shoes. I had chosen rainbow checked Vans. She hated them. She would even run away when I tried to try them on her. She exchanged them for Vans with pictures of uni-Corgis (picture that) and popsicles wearing spectacles.

After we left the mall, she talked me into sitting outside at our coffee shop. I sipped my iced coffee. Clementine raised her giant chocolate chip cookie to her mouth to take a big bite, forgetting she was still wearing her mask.

I laughed hard and she giggled but then she cried a little because she was embarrassed.

Everyone's in on it, aka
You can't trust anyone without a youtube channel aka
There's a conspiracy theorist in every family aka
Brownsound said it best when he wrote "he lost the
election but won the war" aka
Our racist aunts all moved to Parler

Do facts even matter?
I wonder after perusing
popular conspiracies post-election.
Suddenly I recall the enflamed faith
of my childhood, certainty
of mystery, conviction
of seven day creation and
wild animals coupled up
on board an apocalyptic ship.
The terror
of worldwide water
and eternal flame.
Did facts ever matter?

WE MULLED OVER HOW TO MAKE IT NOT A LOST YEAR

I think about what this year could have been.
I sleep over boxes of my unsold books.
We all sleep over some loss.
Let me mourn it.
I want to reach the place of knowing
that I sleep over boxes of promises.
When this ends
promise that we will brush hands again
and crowd around a canvas
our fingers all smudged with pastels.

TO RAISE CHILDREN TODAY IS TO ENGAGE IN MAGICAL THINKING

All three of my children froze this afternoon
from their game playing and negotiations
when I pressed play on another documentary
and the desertification of the world took over the big screen.
Before I could skip ahead they watched waving fields of grass erode
into cracked sand patches and I could see
their dreams of snow melting right through their warm fingers.

On full moon nights
I believe having children is an act of hope
a promise to create world for them, make home for them
an act of intention to keep this thing spinning
to breathe life into entropy, to wild and re-wild

but every other day I damn myself for dooming them
to a world on the brink of extinction.

And yet, when they look
from the bleak screen to me, I can't help it—
I have to believe in each seedlings possibility
the magic of collective action.
Look them in the eyes and say *we're turning this thing around*—see
how I fill the bin with the scraps of my anxiety every day
and cover it with the leaves and the needles
the wind played through
like strings and reeds up in the trees
until they drifted down to rest near the roots
where the girls build fairy houses, scout for caterpillars.

I heap it all in the bin, daily layering in the doom
for which there is simply no space in our small crumb-strewn
house of endless sound and song.
Every spring when the girls have grown bigger
on our incantations of hope
I flip the bin to find what I have made—

Life: warm, rich and resurrecting

P.S.

When we were students, I texted you lets read poetry under the quilt and leave our clothes on the floor by your bed.

Where is home, you asked me long ago when I was spun out in homesickness. We didn't see that we were making it.

Later, when my hormones cratered after the first two babies, I told you don't say nice things to me, I don't deserve them.

Now we are homebodies and we've said a few times, there's no one else I'd want to be shutdown with.

Remember when I lamented that I wouldn't let you love me so poorly? Way back when you slept beside me silent and still and repentant?

Last night under the quilt, we replayed our daughter's laugh that had erupted over and over while we watched Home Alone and I said her laugh was all I needed in this world.

Acknowledgements

Thank you to my writing group, affectionately known as Retired Dentists Quarterly: Jonathan Resendez, Quentin Bell, and Adam Robinson. I wouldn't have created this collection of poems without you.

Thank you to the members of the Holy Family writing group for listening to many of these.

Thank you to Mitch for the support, especially on Wednesdays when I am rushing to prepare for writers group, and for dropping food and drinks off on my desk. Thank you to Anabelle, Clementine, and Beatrix for sharing your lives, words, and ideas with me.

Thank you to Evelyn May at Other Worldly Women Press, Cherie Nelson at The Waking, and Ry Downey and Elionai Zaerahiah at Beatific Magazine for giving a home to several of my poems. And a big thank you to everyone at Finishing Line Press.

Thank you to Colette LaBouff for reading and for your priceless feedback.

Sara Triana is a Texas-based writer of poetry and picture books. She is the author of two children's books, *Love Love Bakery* (2018) and *Every Day is Making Day* (2019), and a chapbook, *Poppy Seeds* (2020). Her poetry and essays have been published in print and online. She lives with her husband and their three daughters near Houston where she enjoys embroidery, being a forgetful gardener, and writing poems in the notes app on her phone outside of the grocery store.

www.ingramcontent.com/pod-product-compliance
Lightning Source LLC
Chambersburg PA
CBHW021151090426
42740CB00008B/1041